T0373572

The Legal Framework of
The European Union

Titles in the Legal Framework Series

The Legal Framework of

The European Union

Leonard Jason-Lloyd

Lecturer in Law, University of Derby, and visiting Lecturer in Law at the Midlands Centre for Criminology and Criminal Justice at Loughborough University and the Scarman Centre for the Study of Public Order at the University of Leicester

and

Sukhwinder Bajwa LLB, LLM

FRANK CASS
LONDON • PORTLAND, OR.

Published in 1997 in Great Britain by
FRANK CASS & CO. LTD.
Newbury House, 900 Eastern Avenue,
London IG2 7HH, England

and in the United States of America by
FRANK CASS
c/o ISBS, Inc.
5804 N.E. Hassalo Street
Portland, Oregon 97213-3644

Transferred to Digital Printing 2004

Copyright © 1997 Frank Cass & Co. Ltd.

British Library Cataloguing in Publication Data

A catalogue record for this book is available
from the British Library

ISBN 0 7146 4291 6
ISSN 0965-3473

Library of Congress Cataloging-in-Publication Data

A catalog record for this book is available
from the Library of Congress

*All rights reserved. No part of this publication may be reproduced in any form
or by any means, electronic, mechanical, photocopying, recording or
otherwise, without the prior permission of Frank Cass & Co. Ltd.*

Contents

1

The Historical Development and Primary Sources of European Union Law

The idea of a unified Europe arose in the aftermath of the horror and devastation of the Second World War. In order to avoid a repetition of such events, it made sense to pull together on a political and economic level in order to create a European community. The initial inspiration for a unified Europe came from a plan devised in 1950 by Robert Schuman (French Foreign Minister) and Jean Monnet, but it is generally accepted that the European Community's most tangible origin was in 1952. It was during this year that a treaty was signed forming the European Coal and Steel Community (ECSC). The participants in this agreement were France, West Germany, The Netherlands, Belgium, Luxembourg and Italy. In 1957 these six nations formed two other mediums for economic co-operation, namely the European Atomic Energy Community (EURATOM) and the European Economic Community (EEC). In effect, there are three European communities which now share the same basic institutional framework (see below).

The primary sources of law within the EC are contained within its treaties. The principal treaty is the Treaty of Rome 1957, which was the document that the original six nations signed on joining the EEC. The document covering membership of the European Coal and Steel Community was the Treaty of Paris, and another treaty signed in Rome instituted the European Atomic Energy Community. Since then a number of additional primary sources of law have been created; this is in addition to the treaties which have been introduced whenever new members join the community.

EXPANSION OF THE COMMUNITY

The first enlargement of the community took place in 1973 with the Accession Treaty, which was signed by Denmark, Ireland and the UK. After its return to democracy, Greece joined the European Community in 1981, followed by Spain and Portugal in 1986. More recently Austria, Sweden and Finland became members on 1 January 1995, expanding the community even further. Turkey, Malta and Cyprus have also applied for membership and it is likely that Malta and Cyprus will become members. Turkey's position is, however, a little more problematic due to its lower level of economic development.

INTRODUCTION OF NEW TREATIES

Other additional treaties of importance include:

• the Merger Treaty 1965.

- the Single European Act 1986.

- the Treaty on European union, agreed in Maastricht on 11 December 1991 (which took effect on 1 November 1993).

The Merger Treaty

The Merger Treaty of 1965 was primarily responsible for establishing a single Council and a single Commission for all three communities. Previously, each community had its own institution. This later proved to be inconvenient and the Merger Treaty, which was implemented on 1 July 1967, combined the three institutions into one.

The Single European Act

The Single European Act was the first amendment to the EC Treaty. It came about as a result of pressure for greater union, and concern over increased competition from North America and the Far East. Its major amendments include:

- Changes in the powers of the Commission.

- Creation of a co-operation procedure, speeding up legislative procedure and giving enhanced legislative powers to the European Parliament.

- Co-operation in the field of foreign policy.

- Co-operation in economic and monetary policy.

- Common policy for the environment.

- Introduction of measures to ensure economic and social cohesion of the community.

- Harmonisation in the field of:
    1. Health
    2. Safety
    3. Consumer protection
    4. Academic, professional and vocational qualifications
    5. Public procurement
    6. VAT and Excise duties
    7. Frontier controls

- Lastly, it set 31 December 1992 as the target date for the completion of the internal market.

Treaty on European Union (Maastricht)

The Treaty on European Union is the most recent amendment to the EC Treaty. This Treaty creates a European union with three pillars including:

- Common foreign and security policy.

- Home affairs and immigration.

- Justice policy.

The Treaty on European Union (TEU) is responsible for the renaming of the European Economic Community as the European Union, thus reflecting the fact that the community is not just concerned with pulling together on an economic level but also intends to integrate on social and political issues. In addition, the TEU brings about important changes to the powers of the community's institutions (see later chapters), and it sets out the procedure and timetable for creating economic and monetary union (EMU). The Treaty contains a number of opt-out provisions, and several member states have taken advantage of these. Denmark, Ireland and the UK have all opted-out of certain provisions; the

UK, specifically, has opted-out from the third stage of the EMU programme.

The Treaty of Rome marked the beginning of the EC and it can also be broadly described as its constitution, since it contains the overall objectives of the community. However, this Treaty now has to be read in conjunction with the changes introduced by subsequent treaties, particularly the TEU.

THE DEVELOPMENT OF GENERAL PRINCIPLES IN EC LAW

The European Community and its legal system have no parallel either past or present, and as time progresses and new treaties are introduced the development of the EC engenders a sense of both excitement and uncertainty. There are two main sources of EC law: namely, primary and secondary sources. Primary sources of EC law stem from the various treaties discussed above. Secondary legislation consists of regulations, directives and decisions. In addition, the EC has developed general principles which are used as a guide to help interpret EC law. These general provisions cannot, however, prevail over any provisions laid down in the treaties. Nevertheless, general principles have become an important tool to aid interpretation and challenges to EC law.

The general principles include:

1. Fundamental rights.

2. Proportionality.

3. Equality.

4. Legal certainty.

5. Procedural rights.

Fundamental Rights

Respect for fundamental rights now forms an integral part of the general principles of law. This concept of respecting fundamental human rights is closely associated with natural justice. The classes of rights that the European Court of Justice have recognised as fundamental include respect for property rights *(Nold v. Commission 4/73 [1974]* ECR 491), religious rights *(Prais v. Council 130/75 [1976]* ECR 1589) and the right to family life *(Demirel v. Stadt schwabisch Gmund 12/86 [1987]* ECR 3719).

Proportionality

This is based on the principle that the 'punishment must fit the crime'. The key question posed is whether the same aim could have been achieved by a method which does not infringe EC law? If there are alternative routes available and these are not adopted, then the method used is disproportionate. If a result can be achieved by a route that does not infringe EC law, that route should be used, thereby making the measure proportionate.

Equality

This principle expects similar cases to be treated in the same way and if, for some reason, they are treated differently, there has to be an objective justification for the different treatment. The concept of equality is further recognised under treaty provisions. For instance, Article 7 of the EC Treaty prohibits discrimination on the grounds of nationality; Article 119 prohibits discrimination on the grounds of sex, demanding equal pay for men and women for equal work; and, finally, Article 40(3) prohibits discrimination between producers and consumers within the community.

Legal Certainty

Legal certainty forms an important aspect of most legal systems. It operates with various subconcepts such as non-retroactivity and legitimate expectations.

Legitimate expectation is a concept derived from German law and basically it ensures that all matters relied on in good faith are respected. Therefore, Community measures must not violate the expectations of the parties concerned, unless such violation is necessary in order to protect the public interest. Thus, if the parties in question firmly believe a particular course of action will be followed and it is reasonable for them to do so, they may then rely on that expectation.

The non-retroactivity principle applies to secondary legislation: namely, regulations, directives and decisions. It prevents a measure from taking effect before its publication. Retroactivity is allowed only if it is necessary to achieve particular objectives and provided individuals' legitimate expectations are respected.

Procedural Rights

Certain procedural rights have been recognised by the EC which include:

1. Right to a hearing (Natural Justice) – a concept adopted from English administrative law.
2. The duty to give reasons (that is, reasons upon which the decision was made).
3. The right to due process.

FIGURE 1

THE STRUCTURE OF THE EUROPEAN UNION

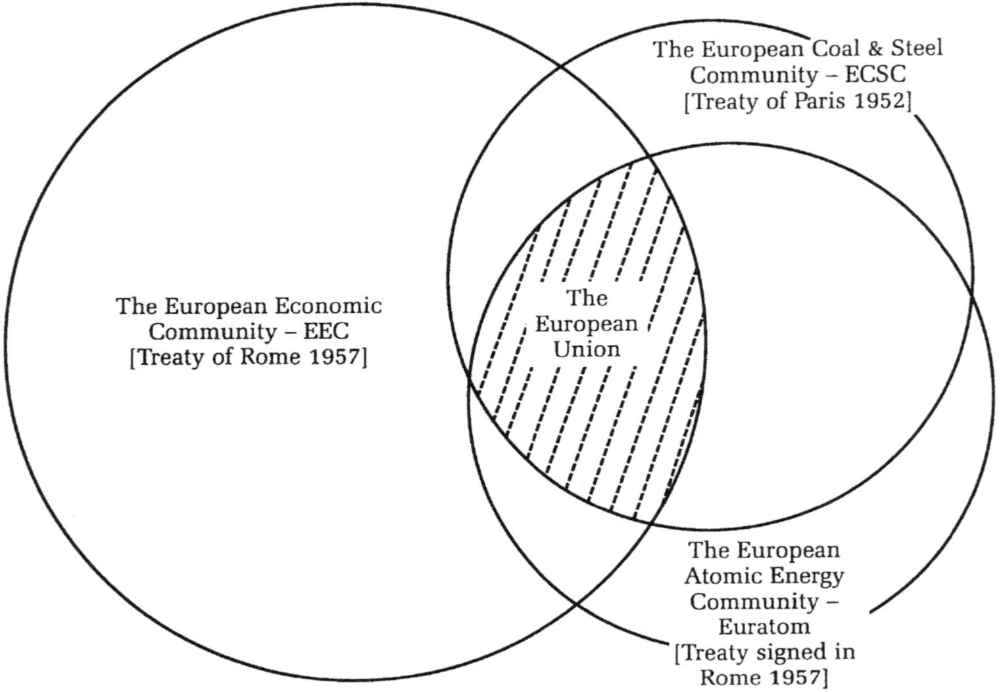

The European Coal & Steel
Community – ECSC
[Treaty of Paris 1952]

The European
Atomic Energy
Community –
Euratom
[Treaty signed in
Rome 1957]

The
European
Union

The European Economic
Community – EEC
[Treaty of Rome 1957]

2

The Institutions of the European Community

THE EUROPEAN COMMISSION

This institution has been defined in many ways – as the executive of the Community and as its driving force and initiator. The Commission consists of 20 members who are appointed by the governments of the member states. France, Italy, Germany, Spain and the UK have two Commissioners and the other states have one each. The aforementioned five nations each have an additional Commissioner because they are the largest states within the EC in terms of population. This factor also has significance when considering the number of seats allocated to each state in the European Parliament and weighted voting in the Council.

Although appointed by agreement of the governments of the member states, the Commissioners are under an obligation neither to seek nor take instructions from any government or from any other body. This is an obligation imposed by Article 10 of the Merger Treaty. Article 11 of the Merger Treaty states that Commissioners must be appointed by 'common accord'. Each appointment must be agreed by all member states and, since the Treaty on European Union came into being, the European Parliament can now veto the appointment of Commissioners. A vital requirement of any Commissioner's function is that they must be prepared to act in the overall interests of the EC and be independent of their respective national governments. Partisan and national loyalties must, therefore, be subordinate to their function within the Commission.

Individual Commissioners can be required to resign on grounds of serious misconduct or the inability to perform properly his or her duties, and the entire Commission may be dismissed by the European Parliament on a two thirds majority provided that a minimum number of its members are present.

The duties of the Commission are numerous and varied. Each Commissioner also has responsibility for at least one subject area (a portfolio). Each subject constitutes an area of activity headed by one of 23 Director-Generals within the Community's bureaucracy, which can loosely be compared to our civil service. The Commission in this respect may therefore be compared to its equivalent institution in Britain, the Cabinet. Individual Director-Generals cover such areas as external relations, economic and financial affairs, agriculture, energy, transport, fisheries, the environment and nuclear safety in addition to personnel and administration. The Commission's bureaucracy comprises about 10,000 personnel who mainly work under the various Director-Generals; there are also approximately 1,500 linguistic employees, in addition to the personal 'cabinet' staff of each Commissioner.

FUNCTIONS

As stated earlier, the Commission is seen as the initiator of the EC, the guardian of EC Treaties, and acts as the Community's executive. This broadly describes its main functions.

Initiator

The Commission has always been seen as the driving force with regard to legislative matters. Generally, Council decisions are taken on the basis of Commission proposals. It is argued that the Treaty on European Union has to an extent diluted the Commission's right to initiative, since the European Parliament, by an overall majority, can now request that the Commission submits proposals. Thus, proposals can be requested by Parliament on matters that they consider require the implementation of a Community measure in order to give full effect to the aims of the EC Treaty. (See Chapter 4 to ascertain what procedure is followed when Commission proposals are rejected.)

The Treaty on European Union introduced three main pillars: common foreign and security policy; home affairs and immigration; and judicial policy. The Commission, together with member states, now shares the right of legislative initiative in respect of common foreign and security policy. In relation to judicial and home affairs, member states have the right of initiative on all matters, while the Commission has the right of initiative in respect of some matters. The Commission also maintains a role in formulating secondary legislation: that is, the issuing of opinions and recommendations which are generally regarded as not legally binding upon member states.

Guardian of the Treaties

The Commission is also known as the guardian or 'watchdog' of the treaties. Its main task is to ensure that the obligations and provisions laid down in the treaties are not violated. If a member state contravenes any of its Treaty obligations, Article 169 of the EC Treaty lays down a procedure for the Commission to follow. First, the alleged offending member state is given the opportunity to explain its case and the Commission then makes its observations accordingly. The Commission may take the matter to the European Court of Justice (ECJ) if the relevant member state fails to remedy the situation within a reasonable time-limit set by the Commission. On average, only about one in seven complaints investigated by the Commission result in the matter being brought before the court. Where it is necessary, such actions are known as 'enforcement proceedings'.

One example of enforcement proceedings occurred when action was taken against the UK in *case 61/81 Commission of the European Communities v. UK of Great Britain and Northern Ireland (1982)* ECR 2601. The UK was declared to be in breach of Article 119 of the EC Treaty and also a Council directive which was enacted to clarify this Article. These two pieces of EC legislation were designed to ensure equal pay for men and women who were doing equal work and, in order that this principle was carried out in practice, the directive contained provision for job-evaluation systems to be used where necessary. The UK duly passed the Sex Discrimination Act 1975 and amended the Equal Pay Act 1970 in order to comply with its obligation under both Article 119 and the relevant directive. However, the UK Parliament fell short of making job-evaluation studies compulsory for employers and refusal on the part of an employer to make such a job evaluation could, therefore, be used to obstruct a claim for equal pay on the part of a woman. In accordance with the procedure outlined above, the Commission gave a reasoned opinion to the UK on this matter and gave the government two months to rectify this anomaly. The UK refused and, under Article 169 of the EC Treaty, the Commission then took action against the UK before the ECJ. In its judgment the court stated that, 'In this instance the UK has not adopted the necessary measures and there is at present no means whereby a worker who considers that his post is of equal value to another may pursue his claims if the employer refuses to introduce a job classification system.' The court went on to declare that the UK had therefore not fulfilled its Treaty obligations. As a result, the Equal Pay (Amendment) Regulations 1983 was passed which enables claims for equal pay to be made even if a job-evaluation scheme has not been effected. In essence, it served to resolve this conflict between EC law and UK domestic law by amending the Equal Pay Act 1970 in order to bring it into line with Article 119 of the EC Treaty and the subsequent directive.

The Commission is also the watchdog for the Community's competition law policy. Under Regulation 17/62 it has the power to impose fines and penalties on individuals for breaches of Articles 85 and 86.

The Commission as the Executive

The Commission is also known as the Community's executive. When a policy decision has been made by the Council, the more detailed implementation of that policy falls to the Commission, who act under powers delegated to it by the Council. The Commission has thus been given wide powers of delegated legislation. The Commission maintains executive powers in the field of:

1. Competition policy (Articles 85–93).

2. Administering the European fund and safeguarding measures (Article 115).

3

The Council

COMPOSITION

Through necessity, the Council is a part-time body since at each meeting it is usually comprised of a representative from each member state. If a specific subject area is to be discussed, the relevant government minister responsible for that area of activity will attend. For instance, if the matter concerns transport, then the ministers responsible for transport from each of the member states will attend. These are called Specialised Council Meetings. However, if a range of issues arise, covering a number of specialised matters, then joint meetings of the Council may sometimes take place.

The Presidency of the Council is conducted on a six-month rotation basis and meetings can be called by either an individual member of the Council, the President, or the Commission. If a government minister is unable to attend, a senior civil servant or ambassador, who is usually a member of the Committee of Permanent Representatives, may attend the Council meeting. However, a permanent representative may not vote, and provision is made, therefore, under Article 150 of the EC Treaty for a proxy system of voting where one member of the Council may ask another to vote in his or her place.

Following a meeting of heads of government at Paris in 1974, the European Council came into being (not to be confused with the Council of Ministers). Article D of the TEU dictates the role and powers of the European Council as providing 'The Union with the necessary impetus for its development and [defining] the necessary political guidelines.'

VOTING

The Council votes in three main ways:

1. Simple majority.

2. Qualified majority.

3. Unanimity.

Under Article 148(1), the European Council acts by simple majority unless the Treaty provides otherwise. Most matters are decided by a qualified majority, with the votes of larger states having greater weight than the votes of smaller states. Under Article 148(2) the voting strength is as follows:

UK, Germany, Italy and France	10 votes each
Spain	8 votes
Belgium, Greece, Netherlands and Portugal	5 votes each
Denmark, Ireland and Finland	3 votes each
Luxembourg	2 votes
Total	79 votes

When enacting a proposal made by the Commission, a qualified majority of 62 is required. It can be seen that the four largest states in terms of weighted votes (the UK, Germany, Italy and France) cannot dominate the Council even if their combined voting strength is augmented by that of Spain, the second largest. Furthermore, certain issues, such as deciding the salaries of the Commissioners, have to receive the minimum of 54 votes, and these must be obtained from at least eight member states.

On rare occasions a unanimous vote is required, but eventually those few Treaty provisions which demand a unaminous vote are likely to disappear and a qualified majority will be substituted. In varying degrees, all these voting procedures ensure that decisions made by the Council will reflect the general will of the member states represented within it.

FUNCTIONS

The European Council's function is to take general policy decisions and to ensure that the objectives set out in the Treaty are attained. Article 145 states that:

It has a duty to ensure co-ordination of the general economic policies of the member states.

The Council has the power to take decisions (which are generally based on Commission proposals), but it is often required to consult Parliament and the Economic and Social Committees. Adoption of the final decision on any legislative proposal rests with the Council, unless the European Parliament vetoes the measure.

COMMITTEE OF PERMANENT REPRESENTATIVES (COREPER)

A major problem inherent within both Councils is their part-time mode of operation. The Committee of

Permanent Representatives, by virtue of its full-time status, therefore exists to reach compromises on the finer points of the relatively broad issues discussed at Council. There are divergent views on the interests that predominate within the Council. Some propound that interests are balanced between national sovereignty and the overall well-being of the EC. Others subscribe to the view that at Council level domestic loyalties take priority. The Committee of Permanent Representatives, by adopting the dual role of representing its own national interests within their EC function and the EC's interests at home, serves to balance this by reaching compromises in cases where national interests compete. There is one permanent representative for each member state and they are appointed by their respective national governments. They are effectively regarded as ambassadors to the EC and are very senior civil servants. COREPER also includes official deputies.

When a proposal is made by the Commission for enactment by the Council, it is scrutinised by COREPER who may, where appropriate, request one of its working groups also to examine it. These working groups are part-time and consist of senior civil servants who have specific areas of responsibility within their respective nations and who represent these interests when required to assist COREPER.

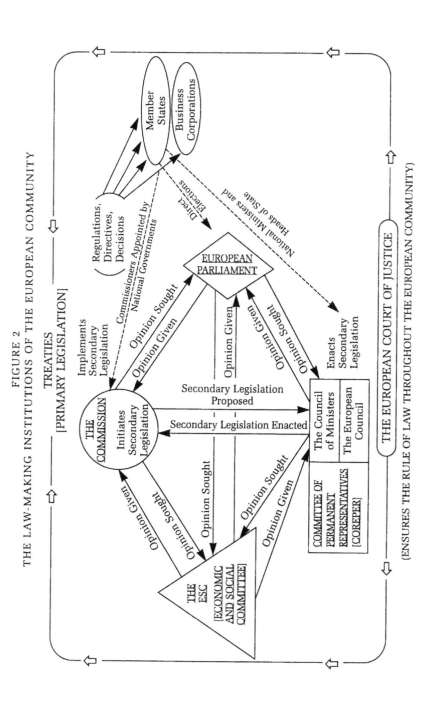

FIGURE 2
THE LAW-MAKING INSTITUTIONS OF THE EUROPEAN COMMUNITY

4

The European Parliament

The word Parliament in this context is misleading since it has no direct legislative power. As seen in previous chapters, this function is vested in the Council. Until 1962 this body was called the 'assembly', which far more accurately described its role within the EC. However, since 1962 the name Parliament has been used and was confirmed by the Single European Act 1986.

COMPOSITION

Although a Member of the European Parliament (MEP) can be a member of a national Parliament, he or she is not allowed to be a member of the government of a member state, the Commission, the Court of Justice, the Court of Auditors, the Economic and Social Committee, the consultative committee of the ECSC, or an active official or servant of any of the Community institutions or a specialised body attached to them, or a Registrar of the Court. In all there are 626 MEPs, made up as follows:

Germany	99
Italy, France and UK	87 each
Spain	64
Netherlands	31
Belgium, Greece and Portugal	25 each
Sweden	22
Austria	21
Denmark and Finland	16 each
Ireland	15
Luxembourg	6

Members are elected for five years. Member states are allowed to use the same election system for their MEPs as used domestically to elect members in their own national legislatures. The UK therefore uses its relative majority vote (or 'first past the post') system, with the exception of Northern Ireland which employs the same form of proportional representation as used in Eire.

MEPs are subject to a number of privileges. They are immune from legal action regarding anything said in the course of their duties, and are availed the same immunities and privileges of their national parliaments during sessions of the European Parliament. Although members of the clergy and peers eligible to sit in the House of Lords are not allowed to sit in our House of Commons, they are permitted to become MEPs. However, anyone disqualified from sitting in the Commons for other reasons will be similarly disqualified from occupying a place in the European Parliament. MEPs from the UK are elected from constituencies much larger than our own national Parliamentary constituencies. This can be seen by simply comparing them with the number of MPs eligible to sit in the House of Commons.

POLITICAL GROUPS

MEPs do not sit in national groups but align themselves with one of the ten multinational political factions that exist in the European Parliament. These political groups include the following in order of numerical strength:

> Socialists
> European People's Party
> Liberals/Democrats/Reformists
> European Democrats
> Greens
> European Unitarian Left
> European Democratic Alliance
> European Right
> Left Unity
> Rainbows

There are also about ten representatives who do not belong to any of these political groupings.

The European Parliament contains a number of committees which have either permanent or temporary status, and cover either general or specific matters. These include the following committees in order of size:

> Political Affairs
> Economic Affairs/Monetary Affairs/Industrial
>   Policy
> Environment/Public Health/Consumer Protection
> Agriculture/Fisheries/Rural Development/
>   Co-operation
> Institutional Affairs
> Social Affairs
> Employment/Regional Planning
> Energy/Research/Technology
> Legal Affairs/Citizens' Rights

Women's Rights
Budgets
Youth/Culture/Education/The Media/Sport
Transport/Tourism
External Economic Relations
Budgetary Control
Rules of Procedure/Verification of Credentials/
    Immunities
Petitions

These committees maintain essential contact with the Commission and the Council when the European Parliament is not in session. A Secretary-General, who is roughly equivalent to the Clerk of the House of Commons, heads a staff of over 3,000 which forms the Secretariat of the European Parliament. A President and 14 Vice-Presidents, who are elected by the European Parliament, constitute its Bureau, which determines Parliament's internal affairs. This Bureau can be enlarged when necessary in order to organise the sessions and agenda of Parliament (assisted in this task by the Secretariat).

FUNCTIONS

The functions of the European Parliament are as follows:

1. Supervisory

2. Legislative

3. Budgetary

Supervisory

The Parliament's supervisory power is exercised over

the institutions in four main ways:

1. Censure

2. Questions

3. Committees of inquiry

4. Legal proceedings

Parliament exercises power over the Commission by having the ability to censure it, thereby obliging the Commission to resign. However, even though Parliament can insist on the resignation of the Commission, that Commission would continue until a new body was appointed by the governments of the member states. Before the TEU, Parliament had no say in the appointment of a new Commission. The TEU has now strengthened Parliament's power by allowing it a power of veto over the appointment of Commissioners.

MEPs and Parliament may question both the Council and the Commission. However, while the Commission is required to reply to questions from Parliament, the Council is not. Although the Council is not obliged to report to Parliament, the President of the European Council does so every six months, submitting a written report on progress towards European union. The TEU now makes these reports obligatory, and the amendments made to the Treaty of Maastricht require Parliament to be informed on several additional matters within the Council concerning economic convergence.

Parliament may also establish committees of inquiry to investigate alleged contravention of EC law or incidents of maladministration.

Under Article 175 Parliament has *locus standi* (the right to bring an action) in the European Court of Justice against the Council and Commission for failure to act. The Maastricht Treaty has also given Parliament the right to initiate legal proceedings under Article 173, but this privilege only applies where the action is to protect its own prerogatives.

Additional supervisory powers given to Parliament under the TEU include the following:

• Parliament has the right to set up temporary committees of inquiry to investigate any breaches of EC law or maladministration in the implementation of Community law.

• The European Parliament can be petitioned by any citizen of the union or resident of a member state on a matter within Community competence which affects him/her directly.

• Parliament is to appoint an ombudsman whose task is to deal with complaints concerning mal-administration in the activities of community institutions or bodies (except the European Court of Justice and the Court of First Instance).

Legislative

Parliament's legislative process occurs in four main ways:

1. Consultation

2. Co-operation

3. Co-decision/conciliation

4. Assent

Consultation:

This procedure means that Parliament is consulted on

proposed legislation. Consultation is required by the Treaty in certain areas. These areas have been added to by the Single European Act (SEA) and further extended by Maastricht. The actual procedure is as follows. First, the Commission forwards a proposal to the Council, which then forwards it to Parliament for its opinion. However, this opinion does not have to be followed. The European Parliament has no right to be consulted on proposed regulations but will often express an opinion. Failure to consult Parliament where it is compulsory (e.g., on decisions regarding the Common Agricultural Policy, harmonisation laws and environmental law) will result in a breach of an 'essential procedural requirement'.

Co-operation:

This procedure was introduced by the SEA and gives Parliament a greater role to play in the legislative process. The procedure works as follows. At the end of the first reading on proposed legislation, the Council will adopt 'a common position'. Parliament can either approve the 'common position' or do nothing for three months, in which case the 'common position' will be adopted. If Parliament rejects the 'common position' (by an absolute majority of its members), the Council can still adopt the legislation but only if it acts unanimously. If Parliament proposes amendments, this requires a re-examination of the common position by the Commission. There is no obligation to adopt Parliament's amendments but the re-examined proposal will be sent back to the Council, who may choose to adopt it (by a qualified majority) or amend it (unanimously).

Co-Decision:

This procedure was introduced by the TEU and is

27

designed to recognise the legislative process as a joint task by the European Parliament and the Council. Thus, Parliament is not given direct legislative powers and the Council has the final say.

The procedure under Article 189b is as follows. The Commission sends its proposals to the Council and Parliament. The Council, as stated earlier, adopts a common position, which can be approved, rejected or amended by Parliament. So far, the procedure follows the same route as the co-operation procedure. It is only if the common position is refused, or if the Council refuses to accept Parliament's amendments, that the conciliation committee comes into play. The conciliation committee (on which both the Council and Parliament is equally represented) aims to find an agreement between the Council and Parliament. The conciliation procedure therefore tries to determine the differences between the institutions in order to establish a joint agreement.

Assent:

The SEA introduced the idea of assent and this has been extended by the TEU. It means that the approval of both the European Parliament and the Council is required before a measure is adopted. Originally, Parliament's assent was needed for the admission of new members and for association agreements with third countries, but the TEU has expanded the category of agreements to which it applies to include non-budgetary legislation.

Budgetary Powers

Parliament also has certain powers regarding the EC budget which it can amend, delay or even reject. In the latter instance, this power was used in 1979 and 1984. The Commission draws up a preliminary draft budget and submits it to the Council, which in turn formulates a draft budget and sends it to the European Parliament. Parliament must either amend the non-compulsory expenditure parts of the budget by an absolute majority or propose modifications to the compulsory expenditure within 45 days. Failure to do so within 45 days will be regarded as approval.

5

The European Court of Justice and the Court of First Instance

The European Court of Justice (the ECJ) is basically designed to ensure that the rule of law under the EC Treaty is observed. It performs this role by interpreting and applying the law where necessary.

COMPOSITION

The ECJ, which is based in Luxembourg, is composed of 15 judges appointed by the agreement of the governments of all the member states. Each judge serves a six-year renewable term of office. There are many features about the composition and procedures of this court which are distinct from UK domestic courts. To begin with, judges in the European Court of Justice are chosen on the basis of an unquestionable independence, and they are either qualified for the highest judicial appointments within their respective countries or are recognised as being learned in the law.

As a result, the bench is comprised of both judges and academic lawyers and legal practitioners. The judges elect a president of the court who serves a three-year renewable term.

In order to assist the judges there are nine advocates-general, who have the same qualifications as the judges and who also serve a six-year renewable term. The role and status of the advocates-general can be difficult to grasp since there are no comparative positions within the UK domestic legal system. Their role within the ECJ can be classed as part advocate and part judicial. During court hearings the advocates-general sit on the same bench as the judges. Their unanimous agreement is also required, in addition to that of all the other judges, in order to dismiss a judge. The equal rank and status of advocates-general to that of the judges is further exemplified by the fact that judges sometimes become advocates-general and vice versa.

A further important distinction between the ECJ and the English courts in particular is their use of the 'inquisitorial' system as opposed to the 'adversarial' or 'accusatorial' system used in the UK. Procedures in the ECJ are therefore akin to the systems used on the continent, whereby proceedings take the form of an enquiry or investigation rather than a contest between the parties. This approach, according to Lord Lane in a lecture delivered in Derby in October 1991, has caused our own lawyers significant difficulties when appearing before the European Court of Justice.

PROCEDURE

The nature of the court's procedures places greater emphasis upon written submissions rather than oral argument. Only when there has been an exchange of written pleadings or written observations are verbal arguments submitted in open court before the judges and one of the advocates-general. Following this hearing, the advocate-general will deliver his or her reasoned opinion on the case, which is highly persuasive but not binding upon the court which sometimes departs from such propositions. Not all cases are heard before the full court; most are heard in chambers in front of three to five judges. There are no means by which decisions made by the ECJ can be appealed against, although the court is able to depart from its own earlier decisions and it is also possible to amend the EC Treaty.

A further crucial difference between the ECJ and the English courts is the method used by the former to interpret the law. In applying EC law to individual cases brought before it, the court uses a teleological approach when interpreting the treaties. This is in contrast to the method used by the English judiciary when applying Acts of Parliament to specific cases, which is generally more narrow than the approach adopted by their European counterparts. The much wider approach used by the European Court is necessary because the wording of the treaties is often very broad and generalised. This necessitates a less restrictive method than that used in the English courts, where statutes are interpreted which are relatively more specific in their wording.

JURISDICTION

There are a number of areas in which the ECJ has jurisdiction, although not all cases may be brought directly before it. Due to an increase in its caseload, a new Court of First Instance was established by the Council in 1988. The two most frequent actions that may be brought directly before the European Court of Justice come under the headings of 'preliminary rulings' and 'enforcement actions'. Preliminary rulings are made under the auspices of Article 177 of the EEC Treaty. The word 'preliminary' within this context has been criticised, since proceedings involving preliminary rulings invariably have already commenced in a national court or tribunal. The purpose of such rulings is to obtain a statement on the interpretation of EC law from the ECJ in order to enable the national court or tribunal to make a judgment on a particular case before it. This, of course, only applies when the national body exercising a judicial function is dealing with a matter affected by EC law.

Preliminary rulings are binding upon the national court which made the reference, and it is incumbent upon the relevant member state to take such steps as are necessary to achieve harmonisation between its domestic law and EC law. In effect, preliminary rulings resolve and avoid conflicts between national and EC law and also assist in achieving general consistency in the interpretation of EC law throughout the Community.

However, it must be stressed that the European Court does not actually decide the case referred to it by a national court or tribunal; it only gives a statement of EC law and leaves it to the relevant national court or tribunal to apply this ruling accordingly.

Under Article 170, the European Court has jurisdiction to hear actions brought by the Commission or a member state against other member states who fail to fulfil their treaty obligations. The complaint still has to be directed through the Commission which, under a similar procedure to that used under Article 169, delivers a reasoned opinion, with failure to comply resulting in the case going before the European Court. The only occasion to date that the provisions under Article 170 have resulted in the matter being referred to the European Court is case *141/78 France v. UK (1979)* ECR 2923, where the court supported the Commission's opinion that the UK was in breach of its treaty obligations regarding the size of mesh in its fishing nets.

In addition to the provisions outlined under Articles 169 and 170, a few specific enforcement procedures exist covering the misuse of national security interests in order to evade Treaty obligations, the abolition or modification of illegal subsidies and removal of restrictions on the free movement of goods. These specific enforcement measures are subject to accelerated proceedings.

Judgments delivered as a result of enforcement proceedings are declaratory and are therefore persuasive but not binding upon member states. In the past, a number of such judgments have been met with deliberate defiance and delay. Under these circumstances the matters disputed have been resolved through political compromises and not through any sanctions imposed by the court.

The final aspect of the ECJ to be examined concerns its judicial control over the institutions of the Community. In this respect it may determine either the illegality of specific actions of an EC institution in its legislative function, or its lack of activity where it has a legal obligation to act. Under Article 173 of the EC Treaty, an action under judicial review may be taken against the relevant institution by either the Commission, the Council, any member state and, since the TEU came into force, the European Parliament or European Central Bank. In certain circumstances an individual, in the form of either a natural or legal person (for example, a corporation), may also bring actions under Article 173. Regulations, Directives and Decisions are reviewable, but recommendations and opinions are not challengeable in this way because they are not legally binding. However, any act on the part of the EC institutions can be subject to judicial review if it has legal effect.

Article 173 is augmented by Article 175, which enables member states and EC institutions to bring an action before the court if the Commission or the Council infringe the EC Treaty by failing to act where appropriate.

The European Court of Justice has appellate jurisdiction over the Court of First Instance, whereby it hears appeals from this court only on points of law. In addition, under Article 228 the European Court of Justice is permitted to give advisory opinions on agreements between the European Union and third countries or international organisations.

COURT OF FIRST INSTANCE

Due to an increase in the workload of the European Court of Justice, a Court of First Instance was instituted by the Council in 1988. This court has jurisdiction to deal with cases involving staff disputes between community institutions and their employees, actions to implement the competition rules, and cases applicable to undertakings and matters relating to ECSC and EURATOM. Since the Maastricht Treaty came into force and made amendments to various aspects of the

EEC Treaty, jurisdiction of the Court of First Instance under Article 168a has been altered to allow the Council to transfer any area of the ECJ's jurisdiction to the Court of First Instance, except Article 177 references.

Composition

The Court of First Instance has judges appointed in the same way and for the same term of office as judges in the European Court of Justice. It is usual for the Court of First Instance to sit in chambers of three or five judges, although the full court may preside over the more important cases. However, there are no advocates-general; where necessary one of the judges will serve in this capacity. Generally, the other procedures of this court are the same as those employed in the Court of Justice. Appeals on points of law from the Court of First Instance may be made to the European Court of Justice.

ECONOMIC AND SOCIAL COMMITTEE

This is an advisory committee and must be consulted by the Commission or Council when required. The issues dealt with by this committee include representation for employers, trade unions, consumer groups and the professions.

COMMITTEE OF REGIONS

This is a new advisory body created by the TEU (Articles 198a to 198c). Its task is to put forward opinions

37

on issues which might have particular effect on regions of the Community. The committee consists of representatives of regional and local bodies in the member states.

EUROPEAN INVESTMENT BANK

The main duty of the European Investment Bank is to ensure that there is a steady and balanced development of the common market in the interests of the Community as a whole. Funding for the European Investment Bank is derived from the member states, which put forward capital according to their size. It deals with a variety of issues, such as aiding less-developed regions; carrying out projects of common interest to all member states; developing new projects to improve the establishment of the common market.

COURT OF AUDITORS

The Court of Auditors was given full recognition as an institution by the TEU. Article 206a states that the court's function is as follows:

> The court of auditors shall examine whether all revenue has been received and all expenditure incurred in a lawful and regular manner and whether the financial management has been sound.

FIGURE 3
ECJ PROCEDURE

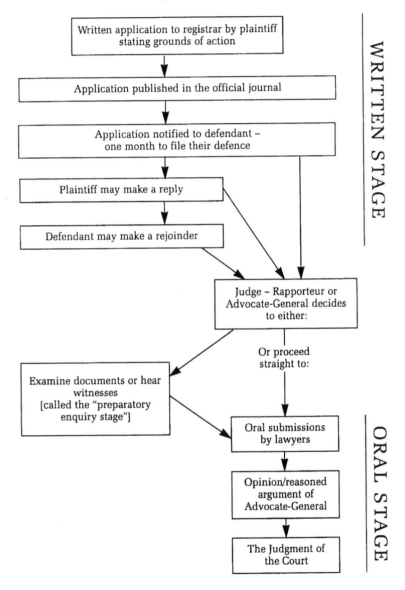

6

Secondary Legislation

REGULATIONS

Regulations are the most prolific form of secondary legislation. In 1988, 434 regulations were enacted by the Council, in contrast to 63 directives and 131 decisions (see below). Once passed, regulations are automatically and directly binding upon all member states and no national legislation is required to put them into operation. This form of secondary legislation is therefore 'directly applicable' (the full meaning and significance of this term will be discussed below). The advantage of regulations is that they can promptly impose precise and consistent rules upon all member states and are binding in their entirety.

One example is Council Regulation 1463/70 which, following the UK's defiance in implementing it, resulted in enforcement proceedings being taken against this nation. In this instance, the regulation in question stipulated that tachographs be compulsorily installed in certain commercial vehicles in order to record the general operation of each conveyance. The UK refused to adopt this rule in its entirety on a number of grounds, one of which centred around fears of a national strike by transport workers, some of whom regarded a tachograph as a 'spy in the cab'. The unions viewed them as an exploitative device used by employers against their members. In accordance with the procedure outlined in Chapter 2, the Commission gave a reasoned opinion on the matter and stated that the provisions of Regulation 1463/70 should be fully complied with. However, the UK failed to implement the scheme within the time-limit specified. As a result, enforcement action was taken before the European Court of Justice by the Commission under *case 128/78 Commission of the European Communities v. United Kingdom of Great Britain and Northern Ireland (1979)* ECR 419. The court ruled that the UK was in breach of its treaty obligations by failing to comply with the relevant regulation and was therefore not allowed unilaterally to avoid its full provisions.

DIRECTIVES

Directives are also binding upon all member states but do not stipulate exact measures to be taken. This is either due to the difficulties involved in specific nations effecting such measures or because it is unnecessary for precise rules to be followed. Directives therefore state general objectives to be reached, while it is left to individual member states to use their own legislative procedures to achieve this end. However, the measures contained within directives must be enacted or administratively implemented, both in their entirety and within set time-limits.

Failure on the part of individual member states to comply with this form of secondary legislation, on grounds of difficulties incurred by its implementation, is unacceptable. One of the main neutralisers of such arguments is that all EC nations participate in the formulation and enactment of directives and, indeed, all secondary legislation (see Chapters 2 to 5). Failure by a member state to fulfil its Treaty obligations, by not implementing a directive either in whole or part, is subject to the same enforcement proceedings initiated by the Commission and subsequently the Court of Justice, as described earlier.

DIRECT APPLICABILITY AND DIRECT EFFECT

It is important at this stage to discuss these two concepts as applied particularly to regulations and directives. As mentioned earlier, a regulation is 'directly applicable', since it becomes immediately legally binding, uniformly and in its entirety, upon all member states. It is not necessary for member states to pass any domestic law in order to implement a regulation. However, regulations may also have 'direct effect', meaning that they can create issues of individual rights of natural or legal persons that must be protected by national courts or tribunals. Furthermore, direct effect is not exclusive to regulations, since it has been held that directives and parts of the EC Treaty may also have direct effect. For example, in *case No. 2 43/75 Defrenne v. Sabena (1976)* ECR 455 it was stated that:

> Article 119 of the EC Treaty states the principle that men and women should get equal pay for equal work.

Ms Defrenne claimed that male air-stewards were getting paid more than female air-hostesses, although carrying out the same tasks. An action was brought claiming that the differences in pay amounted to a breach of Article 119. The key question was whether Article 119 was directly effective. The courts had found, in the earlier case of *Van Gend en Loos 26/82 (1963)* ECR 1, that treaty articles can have direct effect where the action is one which affects the relationship between the state and its individuals; this is an example of what is known as 'vertical effect' (the full meaning of this term will be discussed below).

However, the action in Defrenne, under Article 119, concerned the relationship between individuals and therefore did not amount to having direct effect; this constitutes an example of 'horizontal direct effect'. It was held, however, that Article 119 was directly effective, and that direct effect was not limited to public authorities/the state (as in the Van Gend en Loos case), but that it also covered the relationship between individuals.

The case law cited above illustrates the fact that Treaty Articles are capable of having 'direct effect' (both vertical and horizontal). Regulations, under Article 189, are said to be of 'general application', binding in their entirety and directly applicable in all member states. They take effect, therefore, without the need for further implementation. Thus, regulations are designed to have direct effect and are capable of being invoked either vertically or horizontally. The issue of direct effect in relation to directives is a little more problematic.

A useful case with which to demonstrate how directives may have direct effect is *Van Duyn v. Home Office 41/74 (1974)* ECR 1337. Article 48 of the EC Treaty covers general freedom of movement for workers within the EC, although matters of public policy, security or health may fall outside the ambit of this measure. However, Article 48 was augmented by Council Directive 64/221, which provides that only the personal conduct of the individual concerned shall be used to justify measures taken on grounds of public policy or security. In this case, a Dutch national was refused entry into the UK because she intended to work for an organisation that was considered by the government to be harmful. Action was brought before the High Court in England which in turn, under Article 177 of the EC Treaty, referred the matter to the European Court for a preliminary ruling (see Chapter 5). The European Court ruled that Council Directive 64/221 enabled individual's rights to be enforced in the UK courts, but it went on to say that in this case personal conduct could be related to present association with certain organisations.

The issue of direct effect also requires analysis in relation to whether it is 'vertical' or 'horizontal'. The above case regarding the Dutch national involved the 'vertical' category of direct effectiveness, where a directive may be relied upon by an individual against a member state, including public authorities or other organs of the state. Horizontal direct effect allows a person to bring an action against other individuals or corporations. It was accepted that directives may have direct effect vertically against the state, provided that the conditions under which a directive can have direct effect are satisfied. These conditions are that directives have to be:

1. Sufficiently clear and precise

2. Unconditional

3. Leave no room for discretion in implementation.

The issue of whether directives can have horizontal

effect was addressed in the case of *Marshall v. South West Hampshire Health Authority 152/84 (1986)* ECR 723. Here, the court ruled out any hope of deciding that horizontal direct effect applied to directives. The case was concerned with Directive 76/207, which prohibited sex discrimination at work. The ECJ ruled that the directive may be relied upon against a state authority that is also acting as an employer. In this instance, Miss Marshall worked for a health authority which retired her at 62. She took the matter to an industrial tribunal and then to the Court of Appeal, since she wanted to work until the age of 65, the compulsory retirement age for men. Her action was successful because the health authority was a state organ acting in the capacity of an employer. If, however, a Treaty obligation affects individuals (natural or legal persons), then it has 'horizontal' effect and cannot be enforced in matters between individuals. This view is reinforced in the case of *Duke v. Reliance Systems Ltd (1988)* 2 WLR 359, where a similar case to the above failed because the female employee, who was compulsorily retired at 60, had worked for a private firm.

Thus an individual can only bring an action or challenge a directive if it is against a publicly owned or publicly run enterprise (i.e., 'emanation of the state'). A state employee, according to the Marshall case cited above, can rely on a directive against their employer, but a private employee cannot. Subsequent case law, such as *Foster v. British Gas (1990)* ECR I-3313, helped to clarify what the courts meant by the term 'emanation of the state', and what exactly is seen as a public body or publicly run/owned enterprise. The court held that a directive may be relied on against organisations or bodies which are:

Subject to the authority or control of the state or had special powers beyond those which result from the normal relations between individuals.

At the relevant time, British Gas was still in public ownership.

The ECJ have since attempted to resolve the anomalies between vertical and horizontal direct effect. This has been achieved by allowing individuals to avoid the restrictions laid down in relation to directives having horizontal direct effect, and creating instead an interpretive obligation on national courts. This was a concept introduced in the case of *Von Colson and Kamann v. Land Nordrhein – Westfalen 14/83 (1984)* ECR 1891. This case involved an action by two women seeking remedies in the German courts for unlawful discrimination. They claimed that by refusing to employ the women, who were better qualified than the men, the German prison authorities were in breach of the Equal Treatment Directive 1976. The court did not address the question of whether this was a vertical or horizontal direct effect, but instead turned to Article 5, which requires member states to:

take all appropriate measures to ensure fulfilment of their community obligations.

National courts are, therefore, under an obligation to interpret national legislation in accordance with the aims and purposes of the directive. Thus, the Von Colson principle indirectly achieves horizontal direct effect. This obligation to interpret our own national laws in the light of EC laws has been reflected in more recent case law, such as *Marleasing c-106/89 (1990)* AECR 4135 and *Faccini Dori c-91/92 (1994)* ECR I 3235.

STATE LIABILITY DUE TO FAILURE TO IMPLEMENT DIRECTIVES

The case of *Francovich v. Italy c-6, 9/90 (1992)* IRLR 84 introduced the concept of claiming damages for failing to implement a directive on time. The Italian government failed to implement Directive 80/987, which aimed at giving protection to workers on the insolvency of their employers. Member states were expected to ensure that employees' claims, arising from the employment relationship and relating to pay, were guaranteed. Mr Francovich was unable to enforce a judgment against his employers, and so claimed against the Italian government for failing to implement a directive from which he clearly would have benefited. The ECJ held that damages are available against the state for failure to implement EC directives. The ECJ also laid down three conditions which have to be fulfilled before a member state may be held liable:

1. That the result required by the directive includes the conferring of rights for the benefit of individuals;

2. That the content of those rights is identifiable by reference to the directive;

3. That there exists a causal link between the breach of the state's obligations and the damage suffered by the person affected.

DECISIONS

Although decisions are sometimes classed as secondary legislation, they are by nature more administrative than legislative. However, they occasionally create legal obligations and can be legislative in their effect. Decisions are binding in their entirety upon all those to whom they are addressed. Unlike directives, EC decisions are addressed to specific member states, or even individuals in the form of natural persons or business corporations, and no discretion is given regarding their implementation, hence the term 'binding in their entirety'. Due to the binding nature of decisions, they may be challenged before the ECJ under annulment proceedings (judicial review) under Article 173, either by member states, the Council, the Commission or by individuals. If a decision is addressed to a member state, which subsequently fails to comply, then enforcement proceedings will be instituted under the procedure already outlined under Article 169 of the EC Treaty.

OTHER SOURCES OF LAW

Two other important sources of law which need to be mentioned are Recommendations and Opinions. These two sources only have a persuasive effect, unlike Directives, Regulations and Decisions which are legally binding on all member states.

7

The Supremacy of EC Law

The Treaty is like an incoming tide. It flows into the estuaries and up the rivers. It cannot be held back. Parliament has decreed that the Treaty is henceforward to be part of our law. It is equal in force to any statute... In future transactions which cross the frontiers we must no longer speak or think of English law as something on its own. We must speak and think of community law, of community rights and obligations, and we must give effect to them.

Lord Denning MR (in *Bulmer v. Bolinger 1974*)

The United Kingdom became a member of the European Community initially by signing the Treaty of Rome and subsequently by passing the European Communities Act 1972, which took effect on 1 January 1973. This statute is the means through which EC law is linked with our own national law. As mentioned earlier, some EC law becomes effective in its entirety, without any intervention by member states, and automatically becomes part of their national law. On those occasions where this does not apply, EC law becomes domestic law either by statutory instrument or by Act of Parliament under the auspices of the European Communities Act 1972.

In a nutshell, where there is a conflict between EC and UK law, it is the former that prevails. However, this only applies where the two conflict; EC law does not supplant UK law but exists alongside it. This is the essence of sections 2(4) and 3(1) of the European Communities Act 1972 which state, respectively, that provisions under the Treaty shall, where appropriate, be enforced as law here, with statutes, past and present, being construed accordingly, and that the European Court shall be the final arbiter in any conflict between EC and UK law. One example of how conflicts between the two can be resolved can be seen in the following case study.

In *Macarthys Ltd v. Smith 129/79 (1979)* ECR 1275, a male was employed in a stockroom and paid £60 per week. When he left, a female replaced him who was paid £50 per week. She took the case to an industrial tribunal, claiming that she was entitled to the same pay as her male predecessor in accordance with the Equal Pay Act 1970. Her employers argued that this Act only covered females performing the same work as males if they were working together at the same time. In this instance, the male in question had already left the firm. However, Article 119 of the EC Treaty stated that men and women were entitled to equal pay for equal work and that they did not have to be working together at the same time. In view of this conflict between UK and EC law, the case was referred to the European Court of Justice for a preliminary ruling under the provisions of Article 177. The ECJ subsequently found in favour of the female employee and, in order for UK law to be brought in line with EC law in this respect, the Equal Pay Act 1970 was amended by the Equal Pay (Amendment) Regulations 1983. Sometimes conflicts between UK and EC law have been resolved using other methods, such as judges giving statutes a wide interpretation. Either way, EC law prevails if there is a conflict between them.

Subsequent case law reinforces the view that EC law is 'superior' to our national domestic law and that Community law has priority whenever inconsistency between the two arises. In *Garland v. BREL 12/81 (1982)* ECR 359, inconsistency arose again between UK and EC law. In this instance, a complaint by Mrs Garland had been made against the practice of allowing the families of male ex-employees of BREL concessionary rail-travel facilities after retirement, while families of female ex-employees were not able to enjoy this benefit. Thus, a claim of discrimination under the Sex Discrimination Act 1975 was made. However, under section 6(4) of the Act, any provisions in relation to retirement were exempted from the rules on sex discrimination. Mrs Garland, unable to find assistance from UK law, turned to Article 119 of the EC Treaty. It was held that section 6(4) was inconsistent with the requirements of Article 119 and that Mrs Garland could therefore pursue her claim. Again, this confirms the supremacy that Community law has over our national law.

Later cases seem to have gone a step further in order to give effect to community obligations. For example, the case of *Pickstone v. Freemans Plc (1988)* 3 CMLR 221. This concerned interpretation of the UK's 1983 regulations, which amended the Equal Pay Act 1970 to give effect to obligations under Community law. The courts went one stage further in their approach, by interpreting the regulations against their literal meaning so that they would comply with EC law. It was held that such national legislation must be interpreted 'purposively', to give effect to the broad intentions of Parliament. This meant that their Lordships were prepared to read certain words into the provision, even if this entailed a departure from the strict and literal application of the words used by the legislature. By adapting this method of interpretation, a result compatible with a Directive could be achieved, thus showing a willingness to give effect to Community law.

The case which is seen as a landmark decision and gives an important statement in relation to the supremacy of Community law is *R v. Secretary of State for Transport, ex parte Factortame Ltd No. 2 c-221/89R (1991)* ECR I-3905. In this case, the UK wanted to protect the British fishing quotas under the European quotas system. An Act was passed in 1988 which was designed to stop the practice of quota evasion by Spanish-owned vessels registered in the UK. The new rules prevented many Spanish vessels, previously registered as British, to qualify for registration and they were thus unable to share the UK catch quota. The issue was whether the 1988 Act could be challenged by the Spanish fishermen and, furthermore, whether it was compatible with Community law. The vessel owners sought an injunction against the Crown not to apply the regulation and the House of Lords made a reference to the ECJ. The ECJ held that, where a national court is hearing a case which involves Community law, if that court feels the only reason preventing it from granting interim relief is a rule of national law, then it must set aside the rule. The court also stressed that any Act of Parliament passed after

1972 must be read as subject to directly enforceable Community rights. Thus, the ECJ ruled that the nationality provision of the 1988 Act was illegal and discriminatory under European Union rules.

This ruling is of great significance and further informs us about the implications we face as part of the European Community. Recently, the Factortame case has once again raised issues of obligations faced under EC law. This time the Spanish fishermen are pursuing a claim for damages which has been upheld by the advocates-general. It is expected that the European Court will follow the preliminary and non-binding opinion of the advocates-general when delivering its final verdict.

There has been a constant debate about the extent to which the UK has lost its sovereignty by joining the European Community. The Factortame case has further inflamed this debate. While the issue in its entirety falls outside the scope of this book, it is sufficient to say that our loss of sovereignty should be weighed in conjunction with the benefits of belonging to the EC. It should also be remembered that the other member states have similarly relinquished part of their sovereignty, and that the UK has an equal measure of strength in formulating and influencing EC law as has its three counterparts, Germany, Italy and France, which together with the UK constitute the 'big four' within the European Community.

8

European Community Law in Action

THE COMMON MARKET
(Free Movement of Goods)

Article 9 lays down the foundations of working towards a customs union. However, the actual mechanisms by which the free movement of goods can occur within the EC are those EC Treaty provisions covering the following areas:

Article 12: Prohibits member states from introducing between themselves any new customs duties (on imports or exports), or any charges having equivalent effect, and from increasing those which they already apply in their trade with each other.

Article 95: Prohibits member states from imposing, directly or indirectly, on the products of other member states, any internal taxation of any kind in excess of that imposed directly or indirectly on similar domestic products.

Article 30: Prohibits the use of quantitative restrictions on imports and all measures having equivalent effect

(Article 34 prevents the same with regard to exports).

Article 36: This allows member states to offer justifications for trade practices contrary to Articles 30 and 34.

In order to assess how the above treaty provisions operate, it is necessary to examine each provision and to refer to the relevant case law which expands on the meaning of each provision.

PROHIBITING CUSTOMS DUTIES (Article 12)

Although the EC is concerned with encouraging free movement of 'goods', this is not a term which has actually been defined by the treaties. Instead, we have to turn to the following case law which gives us a clearer idea of what is meant by the term 'goods'.

In the instance of *Commission v. Italy (re export Tax on Art Treasures) case 7/68 (1968)* ECR 423, the Italian Government placed a tax on the exporting of historical and archaeological articles. They claimed they did this in order to protect their artistic heritage. The ECJ rejected the purpose of the tax since they felt that its intention was irrelevant. The key point is that if the products can be valued in money, and can be subject to commercial transaction, then they are classed as 'goods'.

However, goods need to be distinguished from services and capital and later case law sought to do this. If the definition of goods from *Commission v. Italy* was applied to the facts of *Guieseppe Sacchi 155/73 (1974)* ECR 409 then, in theory, television signals could be said to be an item providing a form of payment. They could, therefore, potentially be subject to commercial trans-actions and could be classified as 'goods'. The ECJ, however, felt that the transmission of television signals came within the rules of the treaty relating to services. They are not, therefore, 'goods'. It would seem that the ECJ considers services to be services unless Community law expressly states otherwise.

In the case of *R v. Thompson 7/78 (1978)* ECR 2247, the ECJ had to decide if coins made before 1947 were goods or capital. The ECJ held that if the coins were still used as legal tender, they should be considered as a means of payment and not as goods. In this instance, the coins were not in circulation as legal tender and therefore fell into the category of goods as defined in *Commission v. Italy.*

Article 12 talks in particular about prohibiting new customs duties, or charges which have equivalent effect. It is relatively easy to detect a customs duty, but a charge having an equivalent effect is a little more difficult. However, assistance can be drawn from case law such as *Commission v. Luxembourg and Belgium (Gingerbread) 3/62 (1962)* ECR 425, in which the Court of Justice held that a duty may be considered a charge, having equivalent effect to a customs duty, provided it fulfils the following criteria:

1. It must be imposed unilaterally at the time of importation or subsequently.

2. It must be imposed specifically upon a product from a member state to the exclusion of a similar national product.

3. It must result in an alteration of price and thus have the same effect as a customs duty on the free movement of products.

The courts have also stressed through case law that, in order for a charge to breach Article 12, they are concerned with effect, not purpose or intent. For example, in the case of *Sociaal Fonds Voor de Diamantarbeiders cases 37 and 38/73 (1973)* ECR 1609, a Belgian law required a percentage of the value of imported diamonds to be paid into a social fund for the benefit of workers. It was held that this amounted to having the effect of a customs duty (prohibited under Article 12). The intention or purpose for the charge was irrelevant; and the court held that any pecuniary charge imposed on goods, by reason of the fact that they cross frontiers, would be an obstacle to the free movement of goods. On reaching its decision, the court was concerned with the effect and not the purpose of the charge.

Furthermore, charges which are said to be fees for services rendered have also been classified as contrary to Article 12, as in the case of *Ford Espana SA v. Spanish State 170/88 (1989)* ECR 2305. If, however, the service is required under EC law and it is one which gives a benefit to the importer, then the charge may be justified.

TAXATION (Article 95)

The most popular disguise that a customs duty takes is taxation. If a fee is imposed by a member state on imported goods and it is a measure of internal taxation, it cannot be a charge having equivalent effect and cannot be caught by Article 12. The European Court has developed a new Article 95, under which the issue of genuine taxes is considered. If the tax is not genuine then it will be considered under Article 12. Again, the treaties themselves have not defined the term 'taxation'. This is defined in case law such as *Commission v. France re Reprographic Machines 90/79 (1981)* ECR 283. Here, taxation was defined as a general system of internal dues applied systematically to categories of products in accordance with objective criteria, irrespective of the origin of the products. Taxes that fall within this definition are governed by Article 95. There are two aspects of Article 95 that need to be considered:

Article 95(1) prevents discriminatory taxation on imported goods which are 'similar' to domestic produced goods.

Article 95(2) prohibits member states imposing taxation on the products of other states to give indirect protection to other products. The goods need not be similar but need to be in competition with each other.

Again, in order to assess what is meant by the term 'similar', we need to turn to the relevant case law. It would seem from the case of *Commission v. France re French Taxation of Spirits 168/78 (1980)* ECR 347, that it is not necessary for goods to be identical, but the important question is whether the products have similar characteristics and meet the same needs from the point of view of consumers. In the case of *John Walker 243/84 (1986)* ECR 875, the comparison was between fruit liquor wines and whisky. The ECJ felt that, in order to be considered similar under Article 95, both products had to be more than just alcoholic. What was needed to contravene Article 95 was for alcohol to be present in more or less equal quantities. Since whisky contains more alcohol than fruit liquor wines, it was not similar under Article 95.

The case of *Commission v. UK re Excise Duties on*

Wine 170/78 (1980) ECR 417 involves discussion of Article 95(1) and (2). The issue concerned the competitive relationship between wine and beer. On analysis they were held not to be similar products since it was claimed that:

a) They are produced differently.

b) One is stronger than the other.

The court claimed that Article 95(2) might have been violated and that indirect discrimination might have occurred. In order to prove this, it had to be shown that the two products were in competition and that a higher tax on wine indirectly benefited beer producers in the UK. In order to assess this, the courts felt it was necessary to examine the present state of the market and also the possible developments. After assessing the state of the market, the court held that the two products were in competition and that the higher tax on wine made it a luxury for those who could afford it, thereby benefiting beer producers in the UK.

It seems that indirect discrimination may also occur despite the intent of the parties. If the result is bias to domestic goods, case law suggests that indirect discrimination under Article 95(2) occurs. For example, the case of *Humblot v. Directeur des Services Fiscaux Case 112/84 (1985)* ECR 1367, which involved two types of taxes on cars. The key result was that this tax benefited cars made in France because a higher tax was imposed on cars that were manufactured exceeding 16cv. The French manufacturers escaped this tax since no cars exceeding 16cv were made in France. Thus, it was held to amount to indirect discrimination, contrary to Article 95 (2).

The state may, however, justify indirect discrimination

as shown, for instance, in the case of *Chemical Farmeceutici v. DAF 140/79 (1981)* ECR 1. Here, the Italians had an objective justification for placing a higher charge on a specific form of alcohol. This did not amount to discrimination, as the tax fell within a broader government policy of encouraging the use of agriculturally produced products (felt by the ECJ to be a valid economic aim). This type of justification can only be invoked when indirect discrimination is an issue, hence it is not applicable to direct discrimination.

QUANTITATIVE RESTRICTIONS (Article 30)

Article 30 prohibits quantitative restrictions and all measures having equivalent effect on imports. Clearly, it is necessary to establish what is meant by the term 'quantitative restrictions'. In the case of *Geddo v. Ente Nazionale Risi 2/73 (1973)* ECR 865, quantitative restrictions were described as: Any measures which amount to a total or partial restraint on imports/exports or goods in transit. Subsequent case law has found that bans (as in *Commission v. Italy 7/61 [1961]* ECR 317), quota systems (as in *Salgoli SpA v. Italian Minister of Foreign Trade 13/68 [1968]* ECR 453) and, in certain instances, licences (for example, *International Fruit Co. v. Commission 44/70 [1971]* ECR 411) amount to quantitative restrictions.

MEASURES EQUIVALENT TO A QUANTITATIVE RESTRICTION (MEQR)

Defining MEQR has proved a little more complex. However, it is important to detect when a measure will be an MEQR, in order to predict when a breach of Article 30 has occurred. The ultimate starting-point can be found by referring to the Commission's interpretation of Article 30, which can be found in Directive 70/50. This directive divides the measures into distinctly applicable (which are measures that apply only to imports), and measures which are indistinctly applicable (which are measures which apply equally to domestic and imported products).

The ECJ's interpretation of Article 30 is expressed in the case of *Procureur du Roi v. Dassonville 5/74 (1974)* ECR 837. Here, they found the term MEQR to include: All trading rules enacted by a member state which are capable of hindering, directly or indirectly, actual or potentially intra-community trade. This definition has been consistently applied in subsequent case law and came to be known as the Dassonville formula. The definition in Dassonville is wider than that suggested by Directive 70/50, as it seems to be concerned with the actual effect the measure is capable of having on trade, rather than establishing mere hindrance.

WHAT AMOUNTS TO MEQR AFTER DASSONVILLE?

A variety of measures have amounted to MEQR since Dassonville, including price-fixing schemes, national marketing rules and origin-marking requirements. These are just a few examples showing the application of the Dassonville formula.

In the case of *Tasca 65/75 (1976)* ECR 39, the ECJ held that laying down a maximum price, without making a distinction between domestic products and imported products, does not in itself constitute a measure having an equivalent effect to a quantitative restriction. It may have such an effect when it is fixed at such levels that the sale of imported products becomes, if not impossible, more difficult than the sale of domestic products. It can then be seen as MEQR, especially when it is fixed at such a level that those importing can only do so at a loss. In summary, importers should be allowed to compete fairly with domestic prices.

In certain instances, national marketing rules may amount to a breach of Article 30. This may arise if such rules place restrictions on the production, packaging or distribution of goods. For example, in *Commission v. Belgium re Packaging of Margarine 314/82 (1984)* ECR 1543, the requirement by Belgian national rule for margarine to be packed in cubes and in no other form, such as in tubs or rectangular blocks, amounted to a breach of Article 30.

In the case of *Commission v. Ireland (Irish souvenirs case) 113/80 (1981)* ECR 1625, souvenirs which were not manufactured in that country were required to indicate their country of origin. This requirement was held to be a breach of Article 30, as it gave the consumer the opportunity to exercise a prejudice against foreign goods.

THE CASSIS DE DIJON CASE 120/78 (1979) ECR 649

For a long time it was thought that if the measure in question fell comfortably within the Dassonville formula, it amounted to a breach of Article 30, and that the only defences available were those listed under Article 36. However, since the Cassis case, even if a measure falls within the Dassonville formula it will not necessarily breach Article 30 if it is a measure necessary to satisfy mandatory requirements.

The facts of the Cassis case are as follows. A German law laid down a minimum alcohol content of 25 per cent for spirits, including Cassis. This requirement was satisfied by Cassis being produced in Germany. However, in France the alcohol level was only 15 to 20 per cent. The effect of the German measure, although indistinctly applicable (i.e., equally applicable to domestic-produced goods and imported goods), was to exclude French Cassis from the German market. It was held, therefore, that there had been a breach of Article 30.

The Cassis case introduced two important principles. First, the rule of reason and, secondly, the rule of equivalence (or principle of mutual recognition). The rule of reason states that certain measures – though within the Dassonville formula – will not breach Article 30 if they are necessary to satisfy mandatory requirements. The rule of equivalence stresses that there is no valid reason why goods which have been lawfully produced and marketed in one of the member states should not be introduced into any other member state. Since Cassis, it is important to know what type of measure is being dealt with (distinctly or indistinctly applicable). If it is a distinctly applicable measure that is being challenged, the only defence available is to make reference to one of the derogations listed under Article 36. An indistinctly applicable measure, however, has a wider range of defence, as it can be justified by reference to a mandatory requirement, as well as to the derogations under Article 36.

MANDATORY REQUIREMENTS

The next question is what measures are considered to

be mandatory requirements, enabling member states to escape liability under Article 30? Through case law, it can be seen that protection of the environment, protection of the consumer, and protection of national or regional socio-cultural characteristics, have all been recognised as mandatory requirements. In the case of *Commission v. Denmark (re disposable beer cans) 302/86 (1988)* CML3 619, Danish law stated that, in order to import drinks of beer and soft drinks, all member states had to market drinks in special containers. This was an attempt to help efficient recycling. This case laid down the rule that protection of the environment is a mandatory requirement and can, therefore, escape liability under Article 30. However, since the number of drinks imported was minimal, the risk to the environment was small, and thus not enough to justify the special containers. Nevertheless, it was held that national legislation designed to protect the environment may be regarded as justifying intra-community trade restrictions.

Protection of the consumer has also been held to be a mandatory requirement. In the case of *Oosthoek's BV case 286/81 (1982)* ECR 4575, Dutch law prevented the offering of free gifts to purchasers of encyclopaedias. The logic behind the restriction was that consumers might be induced to buy, without being fully aware of the terms of the agreement. The ECJ upheld national consumer protection measures as they protect the consumer from deception and are thus seen as a mandatory requirement.

A more complex area regarding the limits of Article 30 has been in relation to the laws on Sunday trading. In the case of *Torfaen Borough Council v. B&Q plc 145/88 (1989)* CMLR 337, the issue was whether prohibiting shops to open on Sunday amounted to a breach of Article 30. The court found that not opening on Sunday may be justified by coinciding with 'national or regional social-cultural characteristics'. Therefore, provided there is no breach of the principle of proportionality, there is no breach of Article 30. This approach has been confirmed in the case of *Stoke on Trent City Council v. B&Q c-169/91 (1993)* CMLR 426.

KECK (THE MOST RECENT DEVELOPMENT)

An attempt to define the limits of Article 30 was made in the case of *Keck and Mithourd joint cases c-267 and 268/91 (1993)* ECR I 6097. In this case, goods were sold at a loss, which was contrary to French law. It was submitted that French law prevented the volume of sales of imported goods and that it was therefore incompatible with EC law and breached Article 30. The court re-examined the law in this area and held that:

> Certain equally applicable provisions which restrict marketing arrangements are not to be considered a hindrance on trade according to Dassonville provided they affect all traders and all domestic products and imports in the national territory in the same manner.

Such rules would be held to fall outside Article 30. It seems, according to *Keck*, that in order to escape liability under Article 30 member states can comfortably introduce laws on selling arrangements, provided they have the same effect on both domestic goods and imported goods. If the effect is the same, then the national legislation escapes liability under Article 30.

ARTICLE 36

Article 36 provides that Articles 30–34 shall not preclude prohibitions or restrictions on imports, exports or goods in transit, justified on grounds of:

1. Public morality, public policy, public security.

2. Protection of health and life of humans, animals or plants.

3. Protection of national treasures possessing artistic, historic or archaeological value.

4. Protection of industrial and commercial property.

Such restrictions or prohibitions shall not, however, constitute a means of arbitrary discrimination or a disguised restriction on trade between member states.

Public Morality

An example of public morality being invoked can be seen by reference to the case of *R v. Henn and Darby 34/79 (1979)* ECR 3795. This case concerned the prohibition by UK law on bringing pornographic material into the UK which was 'indecent or obscene'. The UK's domestic law prohibited material of this kind if it was likely to 'deprave or corrupt'. Since the rules applicable to imports were different, it was argued that they were discriminatory and were thus in breach of Article 30. However, they were justified under Article 36, as it was felt that member states have the right to determine the requirements of public morality in their own state. The law prohibiting pornographic materials which were deemed indecent or obscene was thus held to be acceptable.

In contrast, consider the case of *Conegate Ltd v. Customs and Excise Commissions 121/85 (1986)* 2 A11 ER 68. This case concerned the importation of inflatable rubber blow-up dolls, which were prevented from entering the UK. It was held that this prohibition breached Article 30 as the UK had no similar prohibition on the manufacture or marketing of such goods in its own territory. It was held that the prohibition was a disguised restriction and a means of arbitrary discrimination and therefore contrary to Article 36.

Public Policy

The leading case in relation to public policy is *R v. Thompson and Others 7/78 (1978)* ECR 2247. This concerned a ban on the import and export of coins minted before 1947. The restrictions placed were justified under Article 36: it was found that the need to protect the right to mint coinage was one of the fundamental interests of the state and that the state can justify any restrictions on public policy grounds.

Public Security

By reference to the case of *Campus Oil 72/83 (1984)* 3 CMLK 544, it is possible to see how public security has been used. Irish rules insisted that importers of petroleum purchase a proportion of their requirements from an Irish state-owned refinery. It was held that such requirements could be justified as it was vital to guarantee the availability of oil supplies. Thus the rules were justified by the public security exemption.

Protection of the Health or Life of Humans, Animals or Plants

There have been attempts to justify several discriminatory measures on this ground, such as health inspection, licences, import bans and tests. In the case of *Duphar v. Netherlands 238/82 (1984)* ECR 523, it was stated that for this ground to be invoked it is important to satisfy three main points. First, the restriction must not be a disguised form of discrimination; secondly, it must be proportionate; and, finally, a real health risk must be proved.

In the case of *Commission v. UK (UHT Milk) 124/81 (1983)* ECR 203, the health justification was invoked but failed. The UK had placed a requirement of an import licence on all importers bringing in milk and also placed restrictions on its marketing. The court found both requirements to be disproportionate. It was felt that it was unnecessary to market the product in such a manner, and that any information they may have gained via the import licence could have been achieved by some other method that did not have an effect on trade.

In some instances, the courts will accept that a requirement of an import licence can be justified on grounds of protecting health, life of humans, animals or plants. For example, in the case of *Commission v. Ireland (re protection of animals) 74/82 (1984)* ECR 317, because the health standards of Irish poultry were exceptionally high, it was thought that the court had to weigh up the inconvenience caused by the financial and administrative burdens against the dangers and risks to animals' health. Therefore, it was held that the licence requirement could be justified under Article 36.

The issue of subjecting imported products to health checks/tests arose in the case of *Commission v. France (re Italian Table Wines) 42/82 (1983)* ECR 1013. Wine coming from Italy into France was subject to severe delays because of tests being carried out to assess whether Italian wines met the French quality standards. The court held that random checks could be justified, but held that the French authorities carried out systematic checks in excess of those made on their own domestic product. This was found to be a breach of Article 36, as these measures were seen as discriminatory and disproportionate.

Protection of National Treasures Possessing Artistic and Historic or Archaeological Value

The only time this ground has been considered is in relation to the case of *Commission v. Italy 7/68 (1968)* ECR 423, where the Italian government attempted to justify an export tax, claiming it was necessary to protect Italy's art treasures. It was held that Article 36 cannot be invoked to justify a tax.

Protection of Industrial and Commercial Property

This ground is the last exception available under Article 36. It is to be read by making reference to Article 222 of the Treaty which provides that: The treaty shall in no way prejudice the rules in member states governing the system of property ownership. EC law will only protect industrial property rights provided the exercise of the right is a protection of its specific subject matter. The specific subject matter of right can be taken as the right to be the first to market the product, but only with the right-holder's consent (see *Centrafarm Cases 15/74 and 16/74 (1974)* ECR 1147). Any further attempts to enforce the right will not be allowed as the right will be exhausted.

THE FREE MOVEMENT OF CAPITAL

Under Articles 67–73 of the EC Treaty, overall provisions are made for the removal of all restrictions on the movement of capital belonging to EC residents within member states, and discrimination on grounds of the party's nationality or place of residence, or the location of capital invested. Also, the credit systems and capital markets within member states are expected to be liberalised where necessary.

While member states are responsible for the stability of their own currencies and balance-of-payments, the economic policy of member states is dealt with by the Treaty under three main headings:

1. Conjunctural policy governed by Article 103.

2. Balance-of-payments governed by Article 104.

3. The Community's commercial policy governed by Articles 110 to 116.

Conjunctural Policy

This is governed by Article 103, which states that member states 'shall regard their conjunctural policies as a matter of common concern. They shall consult each other and the Commission on the measures to be taken in the light of the prevailing circumstances.'

Balance-of-Payments

Balance-of-payments are governed by Article 104, which

states that 'Each member state shall pursue the economic policy needed to ensure the equilibrium of its overall balance of payments and maintain confidence in its currency, while taking care to ensure a high level of employment and a stable level of prices.'

(Articles 105 to 109 maintain responsibility for promoting further common action between member states with regard to economic policy-making.)

Community's Commercial Policy

This is governed by Articles 110 to 116, which require member states to work towards the abolition of restrictions in relation to international trade, and to promote the harmonious development of world trade and lower customs barriers.

THE SINGLE EUROPEAN ACT

This Act has made further additions to the free movement of capital by inserting Article 102a to the title of the Treaty. This provision insists on co-operation among member states in relation to monetary policy. Other provisions aimed at creating free movement of capital have been triggered by secondary legislation in the form of Directive 88/361. This was introduced in an attempt to abolish any remaining restrictions on the movement of capital between persons resident in member states. However, there are exceptions to this, where member states are allowed to take safeguarding measures where short-term capital movements of exceptional size impose severe strains on foreign exchange markets.

Thus, it can be seen how difficult it remains to

achieve total freedom of capital since, despite Directive 88/361, member states can in certain instances impose restrictions on capital. Other developments in this area can be seen by reference to changes brought about by Maastricht. The Maastricht Treaty replaces Articles 67 to 73, enforcing new provisions which are aimed at encouraging total freedom of capital between member states and between the community and third countries. Maastricht is also responsible for setting up the European Central Bank, which will hold authority to issue the common currency that will eventually replace the national currencies of the member states. The move towards achieving a European Monetary System is being approached in three stages. The first stage requires member states to give full effect to the principle of free movement of capital. This includes liberalising their financial institutions and working towards a common economic policy. The second stage involves increased co-operation among national central banks and a greater integration on the issue of monetary policy. The third stage is responsible for the introduction of the single currency, and this is the stage from which the UK has chosen to opt out. The date set to commence proceedings for the third stage is 31 December 1996. It is hoped that the third stage will not be prolonged and it is anticipated that economic and monetary union will commence no later than 1 January 1999.

9

Free Movement of Persons

Holders of passports issued in recent years within the UK will have noticed that the traditional black document has been replaced by a much smaller, burgundy red European Community passport. All member states now issue their passports using the same format and this is designed to assist the movement of EC nationals within the Community. As far as the public is concerned, this is probably one of the most visible symbols of our membership of the European Community.

Under Articles 3 and 48–66 of the EC Treaty (augmented by a number of regulations and directives), freedom of movement covers two categories of persons: namely, workers (employees) and non-employees, such as professional fee-earners and the self-employed, including tradespeople. This chapter is primarily concerned with a discussion of the free movement of workers. Both primary legislation (treaties) and secondary legislation (directives and regulations), dictate the amount of freedom afforded to workers within the community. If we look at Article 48, we can see how the principle of the free movement of workers operates. Article 48(2) states that 'the freedom requires the abolition of any discrimination based on nationality between workers of the member states in relation to employment, remuneration and other conditions of work and employment.'

Under Article 49(3), member states are permitted to restrict the freedom of workers if they can justify it on any one of the following grounds:

1. Public Policy.

2. Public Health.

3. Public Security.

SECONDARY LEGISLATION

Regulation 1612/68 governs access to, and conditions of, employment.

Regulation 1251/70 grants the right to remain in the territory of a member state after employment.

Directive 68/360 grants rights of entry and residence.

Directive 64/221 governs rights of member states to derogate from free movement on grounds listed under Article 48(3).

WHO IS A WORKER?

The Treaty itself does not define a 'worker'. It is, therefore, necessary to turn to case law to ascertain the meaning of this term. It seems that a person can still be considered a worker if, having lost one job, they are seeking employment and are capable of finding another. This was the definition of the term 'worker' in the case of *Hoekstra unger v. BBDA 75/63 (1964)* ECR 177. Subsequent cases have given an even more generous meaning to the term, as in *Levin 53/81 (1982)* ECR 1035, where part-time employment enabled a person to be seen as a worker, providing the work was genuine and an activity of an economic nature. Even if someone is working part-time and receiving supplementary benefit, according to the decision in *Kempf v. Staatsecretaris Van Justitie 139/85 (1987)* 1 CMLR 764, they will still be seen as a worker. The relevant case law suggests that providing a person's job is a genuine and effective activity, they will be seen as a worker. The case of *Lawrie-Blum 66/85 (1986)* ECR 2121 outlines in a nutshell the essential features of an employment relationship and, hence, who is seen as a worker. The essential features include the following:

1. The provision of some sort of service.

2. Being directed by another person.

3. Working in return for remuneration.

REGULATION 1612/68

Regulation 1612/68 aims to deal with granting equality to workers in all matters relating to the activities of employed persons. It is divided into three areas:

1. Eligibility for employment.

2. Equality in employment.

3. Workers' families.

By referring to relevant case law, one can see how the EC has approached the issue of equality towards workers from other member states.

ELIGIBILITY FOR EMPLOYMENT

In the case of *Commission v. France re Merchant Seamen 167/73 (1974)* ECR 359, a requirement in French law stated that the crew of merchant ships should have three French members for every non-French crew member. It was held that such a requirement was contrary to EC law. Thus any national of a member state has the right to take up and pursue activity as an employed person under the same conditions as those imposed on nationals of the host state. Discrimination is therefore prohibited, thereby promoting the principle of free movement of workers.

EQUALITY IN EMPLOYMENT

This refers to being treated equally in relation to conditions of employment, remuneration, reinstatement and re-employment, and not being discriminated against on the basis of nationality. Case law has also indicated (along with Treaty provisions) that migrant workers are entitled to the same social and tax advantages as national workers. Thus, in the case of *Fiorini v. SNCF 32/75 (1975)* ECR 1085, the term 'social advantage' has been given a wide meaning, including the right to a special rail-reduction card to parents of large families. This benefit was granted despite the fact that it was not a benefit attached to contracts of employment. The family in this case, because they were entitled to remain in France under Regulation 1251/70, also had the right to benefit from the provisions of Article 7(2) to equal social advantages.

WORKERS' FAMILIES

As well as the worker being entitled to equal rights and treatment, these rights extend to his or her family members, even if the family members are non-EC nationals. The important question is: who are considered to be members of a worker's family? Members of a worker's family include his or her spouse, and their descendants who are under the age of 21 or who are dependants, and dependent relatives in the ascending line of the worker and his or her spouse. Article 10(2) requires member states to facilitate the admission of other family members who are either dependent on the worker or who lived under the same roof in the state of origin.

The issue which has caused particular concern is the term 'spouse', and whether it extends to include cohabitees and couples who, although still married, are separated. Case law seems to indicate that the term spouse does not include cohabitees. For example, in *Netherlands v. Reed 59/85 (1987)* 2 CMLR 448, the court held that community law maintains that the term spouse refers to marital relationships only. The only reason Ms Reed succeeded in staying in Holland was that Dutch law gives cohabitees the same rights as spouses, provided they can show permanence in their relationship. Therefore, since all other national workers have the benefit of this law, to deprive Ms Reed of it would have amounted to discrimination, breaching Articles 7 and 48 of the EC Treaty.

The issue of whether separation means losing the rights given as a spouse was dealt with in the case of *Diatta v. Berlin 267/83 (1985)* ECR 567. It was held that even though a person may be separated they do not lose their right of residence until the marriage is actually dissolved.

Article 11 grants family members (who have a right to live with the worker) the right to take up any activity as an employed person even if they are a non-EC national. This was shown in *Gul case 131/85 (1986)* ECR 1573, where a Turkish-Cypriot husband of an English woman, working and living in Germany, was denied the right to practise as a doctor, even though he had all the necessary qualifications from Turkey, further qualifications from Germany and had even worked in Germany on a temporary basis in the past. The husband claimed that there had been a breach of EC law. The court stressed that, provided the qualifications were recognised, the spouse of a migrant worker under Article 11 is entitled to practise his or her profession.

Under Article 12, the children of workers are entitled to be treated equally in relation to access to education, apprenticeships or vocational training courses. An example of how Article 12 operates can be seen in *Moritz v. Netherlands Minister for Education case 390/87 (1989)* ECR 723. This case involved a claim for an educational allowance from the Dutch authorities by the child of a migrant worker. His parents had returned to their native country but the child stayed on to complete his studies. It was held that the child does not lose his rights as a child of the family, even if the parents return to their own country, and the child was, therefore, allowed to stay on to complete his course. The same principle applies to spouses. This can be seen by reference to the case of *Forcheri v. Belgian State 152/82 (1983)* ECR 2323. Mrs Forcheri (wife of an Italian EC official) made an application to commence a social-work training course. Her application was accepted on the condition that she paid an extra fee. This fee was payable only by non-Belgian nationals. It was held that Mrs Forcheri, by paying the fee, was being discriminated against, and hence this breached Article 7.

REGULATION 1251/70

This regulation relates to the right of workers to remain in the territory of a member state having been employed there. However, in order to invoke this regulation it is necessary to satisfy one of the following grounds:

1. The worker must be retired: in order to qualify for retirement a person must have worked in the member state for at least 12 months and resided continuously there for the last three years.

2. Incapacitated workers: This applies to people who, due to a permanent incapacity, have to cease employment. However, it is necessary for the worker to have resided in the member state for the last two years.

3. Frontier workers: These are workers who take up employment in another member state after three years' employment and residence in the host state, while continuing to reside in that member state.

Under Regulation 1251/70, members of the worker's family also have the right to remain permanently, providing the worker has the right to remain. If the worker has a right to stay due to any of the reasons quoted above, and if he or she then dies, their family may remain after his or her death. If, however, he or she dies before acquiring rights of residence, then their family are only entitled to stay if:

1. The worker had resided there for at least two years.

2. The worker's death was caused by an accident at work or due to an occupational illness.

3. The surviving spouse is a national of the state of residence or was a national of that state before marriage to the worker.

DIRECTIVE 68/360

Directive 68/360 governs the rights of workers in relation to rights and residence. The directive enables member states to demand proof of a person's status as a 'worker' and hence certain documentation must be shown. The requirement in terms of documentation is a valid identity card or passport. Family members who are not nationals of a member state may be required to show additional documentation. On producing these documents and establishing the fact that they have employment, a worker should have the right of entry and residence.

Although Article 48 grants workers free movement within the Community, there are exceptions to this rule which are defined in Article 48(3) and Directive 64/221.

ARTICLE 48 AND DIRECTIVE 64/221

The justifications for violating the principle on free movement of persons include public policy grounds, public security grounds and public health. Directive 64/221 assists one further in ascertaining when these grounds can be invoked, and states that the measure will be assessed by reference to the personal conduct of the individual concerned; thus previous convictions are not always enough to justify exclusion. The directive also lists all diseases and disabilities which would justify exclusion on the ground of public health. A useful illustration of Article 48(3) is the case of *Van Duyn v. Home Office 41/74 (1974)* ECR 1337, which gives an indication of how to assess personal conduct. In this particular case, a Dutch national was refused entry into the UK on the grounds of public policy. The Dutch national wished to take up employment with the Church of Scientology. The refusal was based on her association with this sect. The ECJ held that the conduct does not have to be illegal to justify exclusion but must be socially harmful; in this instance, association with a socially harmful institution was deemed as current personal conduct.

FREEDOM TO PROVIDE SERVICES

It is a major prerequisite of the freedom to provide services within the European Community that the applicant is pursuing a professional activity. The provisions governing this freedom are contained within Articles 59–66 of the EC Treaty. There are similarities in both the provisions and derogations within the legal framework affecting the right of establishment and freedom to provide services. One fundamental difference, however, is that the latter does not necessarily entail residential rights whereas the former does. Although the Treaty makes provision for providing services, it makes no mention of entitlement to receive services. The European Court of Justice has, since 1975, held that freedom to receive services runs alongside their actual provision. Therefore, restrictions should be removed, for instance, in respect of persons entering EC states as tourists, or for the purposes of receiving medical treatment or education.

With the exception of banking, transport and insurance, which are covered separately under the EC Treaty, the term 'services' has been held to include a host of paid occupations that fall outside the scope of those provisions covering goods, capital and persons. It also encompasses members of the various professions where differences in qualifications and general standards between EC states have been systematically harmonised, particularly in medicine and architecture. Therefore, an EC national who is a member of such a profession will be entitled to practise in any EC state and, possibly, to establish a business there. But not all professions have been harmonised in this way, and traditional rules of conduct within certain professions could still be an impediment to the right to provide services. However, if such rules are discriminatory by nature, or unjustified or disproportionate, they can be challenged before the European Court. Two EC Directives have begun a system of mutual recognition of higher education qualifications between member states, which are primarily designed to expedite the process of recognition.

However, if there are notable differences in standards and procedures in the exercise of the applicant's profession at home compared with the host state, parity may be achieved by either taking an aptitude test or fulfilling an adaptation period, whichever is considered the most appropriate by the host country.

Index

Table of Statutes

Table of Cases

For Product Safety Concerns and Information please contact our EU
representative GPSR@taylorandfrancis.com
Taylor & Francis Verlag GmbH, Kaufingerstraße 24, 80331 München, Germany

www.ingramcontent.com/pod-product-compliance
Ingram Content Group UK Ltd.
Pitfield, Milton Keynes, MK11 3LW, UK
UKHW010813080625
459435UK00006B/57